Nutribullet Superfood

40 Protein Packed Power Smoothie Recipes To Help You Lose Weight And Build Lean Muscle (Includes: Bonus Protein Add-Ins Guide)

by Jessica David

TABLE OF CONTENTS

INTRODUCTION

I want to thank you and congratulate you for downloading Nutribullet Superfood: 40 Protein Packed Power Smoothie Recipes To Help You Lose Weight And Build Lean Muscle. Studies show protein works as a building block for healthy skin, hair, bones, and heart in any person. With a nutritious diet, one will be able to maximize a workout regime

This book contains proven ingredients and recipes that will help you lose weight and build muscle at the same time. Each recipe is simple to make and only requires one thing – a Nutribullet. Stay fit while enjoying blended treats concocted with the most nutritious ingredients on Earth.

Thanks again for downloading this book, I hope you enjoy it!

"I'm too busy to chew. That's why I blend all my meals into smoothies, and I make love as slowly as ice cream melts in the Sahara."

— Jarod Kintz

Almond Blast Smoothie

Ingredients:

- 2 scoops vanilla whey protein
- 1 cup skim milk
- 1/2 cup dry oatmeal
- 1/2 cup raisins
- 12 slivered almonds
- 1 tbsp peanut butter

Preparation:

Prepare all of the ingredients and place them into the Nutribullet. Blend and enjoy.

Apricot Oat and Walnut Smoothie

Ingredients:

- 2 medium apricots
- 1 scoop whey protein powder
- 1 tablespoon rolled oats
- 10g walnut
- 1 cup water

Preparation:

Prepare all of the ingredients and place them into the Nutribullet. Blend and enjoy.

Bahama Bro

Ingredients:

- 1 cup frozen pineapple
- 4 ice cubes
- 1⁄2 cup no pulp orange juice
- 1⁄4 cup coconut milk
- 2 scoops vanilla whey protein powder

Preparation:

Prepare all of the ingredients and place them into the Nutribullet. Blend and enjoy.

Banana Awesome Smoothie

Ingredients:

- 1 cup water (or milk)
- 2 bananas2 scoops protein
- 2 tsp flaxseed oil

Preparation:

Prepare all of the ingredients and place them into the Nutribullet. Blend and enjoy.

Banana Blueberry Health Nut Smoothie

Ingredients:

- 1 tbsp sunflower seeds
- 1 tbsp pumpkin seeds
- 2 cups spinach
- 1/4 cup raspberries
- 1/4 cup blueberries
- 1 whole banana
- 1 cup almond milk

Preparation:

Prepare all of the ingredients and place them into the Nutribullet. Blend and enjoy.

Blueberry Honey Tofu Smoothie

Ingredients:

- 1 tbsp honey
- 1 cup blueberries
- 1 medium banana
- 6 ounce tofu soft
- 1 cup soy milk

Preparation:

Prepare all of the ingredients and place them into the Nutribullet. Blend and enjoy.

Blueberry Pear Smoothie

Ingredients:

- 1 scoop soy protein powder
- 1/2 cup blueberries
- 1/2 medium pear
- 1 cup water

Preparation:

Prepare all of the ingredients and place them into the Nutribullet. Blend and enjoy.

Cabbage Peach Smoothie

Ingredients:

- 1/2 cup cabbage
- 1 medium peach
- 1 scoop whey protein powder, vanilla
- 1 teaspoon flax seeds
- 1 cup water

Preparation:

Prepare -all of the ingredients and place them into the Nutribullet. Blend and enjoy.

Caramel Apple Smoothie

Ingredients:

- 1/2 cup cottage cheese
- 1 scoop vanilla whey protein powder
- 1/2 apple
- 1/2 tsp caramel extract
- 1/2 tsp apple spice
- A pinch of cinnamon
- 5-6 ice cubes
- 1 cup water

Preparation:

Prepare all of the ingredients and place them into the Nutribullet. Blend and enjoy.

Cherry Almond Smoothie

Ingredients:

- 1 cup of pitted cherries
- 1 cup of almond milk
- 2 tbsp of almond butter
- 4 ice cubes
- 1 scoop vanilla protein powder

Preparation:

Prepare all of the ingredients and place them into the Nutribullet. Blend and enjoy.

Chocolate and Peanut Butter Smoothie

Ingredients:

- 1 tbsp peanut butter
- 2 scoops whey protein, chocolate
- 3 ice cubes
- 1 banana
- 1 cup almond milk

Preparation:

Prepare all of the ingredients and place them into the Nutribullet. Blend and enjoy.

Coffee Banana Monkey Smoothie

Ingredients:

- 1 cup brewed coffee
- 1 banana
- 1 cup non fat Greek yoghurt
- 1 tbsp ground flax seed
- 2 tsp honey
- 1/2 tsp ground cinnamon
- 1/4 tsp grated nutmeg
- 5 ice cubes

Preparation:

Prepare all of the ingredients and place them into the Nutribullet. Blend and enjoy.

Creatine Explosion Smoothie

Ingredients:

- 2 scoops vanilla whey protein
- 2 Granny Smith apples
- 1 scoop Creatine powder
- 1 scoop ice

Preparation:

Prepare all of the ingredients and place them into the Nutribullet. Blend and enjoy.

Double Berry Smoothie

Ingredients:

- 2 scoops whey protein
- 4 large strawberries
- 1 cup blueberries
- 1/2 cup water
- 1 scoop ice

Preparation:

Prepare all of the ingredients and place them into the Nutribullet. Blend and enjoy.

Frosty Frozen Smoothie

Ingredients:

- 1/4 tsp vanilla extract
- 2 scoops whey protein, chocolate flavor
- 1/2 tsp xanthan gum
- 1 cup almond milk
- 2 cups ice
- 1 banana

Preparation:

Prepare all of the ingredients and place them into the Nutribullet. Blend and enjoy.

Grape Berry Smoothie

Ingredients:

- 1/2 cup water
- 1 tsp chia seeds
- 1 tsp flaxseed oil
- 2 scoops whey protein, vanilla
- 1/2 cup blueberries
- 1/2 cup red grapes

Preparation:

Prepare all of the ingredients and place them into the Nutribullet. Blend and enjoy.

Green Warrior Protein Smoothie

Ingredients:

- 1/2 cup red grapefruit juice
- 1 cup destemmed dinosaur kale
- 1 large sweet apple
- 1 cup cucumber
- 1/4 cup celery
- 3 tbsp hemp hearts
- 1/4 cup frozen mango
- 1/2 tbsp virgin coconut oil

Preparation:

Prepare all of the ingredients and place them into the Nutribullet. Blend and enjoy.

Hemp Fruit Energy Smoothie

Ingredients:

- 1/2 kiwi
- 1/2 banana
- 1 scoop soy protein powder
- 1 tsp hemp seeds
- 1 cup water

Preparation:

Prepare all of the ingredients and place them into the Nutribullet. Blend and enjoy.

Kale, Banana, Seed Superfood Smoothie

Ingredients:

- 3/4 cup vanilla almond milk
- 1 pitted date
- 1 tbsp raw hemp seeds
- 1 banana
- 1/2 tbsp chia seeds
- 3/4 cup baby kale

Preparation:

Prepare all of the ingredients and place them into the Nutribullet. Blend and enjoy.

Kale, Berry and Acai Power Smoothie

Ingredients:

- 1 banana
- 1/2 cup blueberries
- 1/2 cup strawberries
- 1/2 cup kale
- 1/4 cup almond milk 1 tbsp flax seed
- 1 tbsp hemp powder
- 1 tbsp chia seeds
- 1 tbsp acai
- 1 tsp cinnamon

Preparation:

Prepare all of the ingredients and place them into the Nutribullet. Blend and enjoy.

Kiwi Almond Protein Smoothie

Ingredients:

- 10 almonds
- 1 kiwi
- 2 tbsp oats
- 1 scoop whey protein powder
- 1 cup water

Preparation:

Prepare all of the ingredients and place them into the Nutribullet. Blend and enjoy.

Mineral Power Smoothie

Ingredients:

- 1 cup water
- 1 packet liquid minerals
- 1 packet gelatin powder
- 1 tbsp flaxseed oil
- 1 scoop whey protein

Preparation:

Prepare all of the ingredients and place them into the Nutribullet. Blend and enjoy.

Oatmeal Smoothie

Ingredients:

- 1 cup oatmeal
- 2 scoops vanilla whey protein
- 1/2 tsp cinnamon
- 1/8 cup maple syrup
- 1 tbsp almonds
- 1 cup water or milk

Preparation:

Prepare all of the ingredients and place them into the Nutribullet. Blend and enjoy.

Oats and Banana Smoothie

Ingredients:

- 2 scoops whey protein, vanilla
- 2 ice cubes
- 2 bananas
- 1/4 tsp cinnamon
- 2 tbsp rolled oats
- 1 tsp honey
- 1 cup almond milk
- 1/2 cup water

Preparation:

Prepare all of the ingredients and place them into the Nutribullet. Blend and enjoy.

Papaya Coconut Banana Smoothie

Ingredients:

- 1/2 cup papaya
- 1/2 banana
- 1 scoop whey protein powder, plain or vanilla
- 1 cup coconut water

Preparation:

Prepare all of the ingredients and place them into the Nutribullet. Blend and enjoy.

Peach Sensation Smoothie

Ingredients:

- 1 tbsp flax seeds
- 2 scoops whey protein, vanilla
- 2 cups kale
- 1 cup almond milk
- 1/2 banana
- 1 cup peaches
- 1/2 cup pineapple

Preparation:

Prepare all of the ingredients and place them into the Nutribullet. Blend and enjoy.

Peaches and Cream

Ingredients:

- 2 cups peaches
- 1⁄4 cup Greek yogurt
- 1⁄2 cup orange juice
- 2 scoops whey protein powder, vanilla

Preparation:

Prepare all of the ingredients and place them into the Nutribullet. Blend and enjoy.

Peanut Butter and Jelly

Ingredients:

- 1 cup frozen strawberries
- 2 ice cubes
- 2 tbsp peanut butter
- 1 tbsp strawberry fruit spread
- 1 cup vanilla almond milk
- 1 scoop whey protein powder, strawberry

Preparation:

Prepare all of the ingredients and place them into the Nutribullet. Blend and enjoy.

Peanut Butter Banana Smoothie

Ingredients:

- 2 scoops protein
- 1/2 cup almonds
- 1 tbsp peanut butter
- 1 cup skim milk
- 1/2 banana
- 1 tbsp honey

Preparation:

Prepare all of the ingredients and place them into the Nutribullet. Blend and enjoy.

Pina Colada Smoothie

Ingredients:

- 2 scoops whey protein, vanilla
- 1/2 cup pineapple orange juice
- 1/4 tsp rum extract
- 1/4 tsp coconut extract
- 1/2 cup water or milk

Preparation:

Prepare all of the ingredients and place them into the Nutribullet. Blend and enjoy.

Pineapple Coconut Milk Smoothie

Ingredients:

- 1/4 cup grain oats
- 1 tsp Chia seeds
- 1 cup coconut milk
- 1/4 cup Greek Yoghurt
- 1 cup pineapple chunks
- 2 tsp sugar

Preparation:

Prepare all of the ingredients and place them into the Nutribullet. Blend and enjoy.

Pineapple Power Smoothie

Ingredients:

- 1 cup pineapple juice
- 3 strawberries
- 1 banana
- 1 tsp Greek yoghurt
- 1 scoop whey protein, vanilla

Preparation:

Prepare all of the ingredients and place them into the Nutribullet. Blend and enjoy.

Protein Berry Smoothie

Ingredients:

- 1/2 cup blueberries
- 1/2 cup blackberries
- 1 kiwi, skin intact
- 1 tsp flax seed
- 1 cup Greek yoghurt
- 1 cup milk or coconut milk

Preparation:

Prepare all of the ingredients and place them into the Nutribullet. Blend and enjoy.

Raspberry Banana Energy Smoothie

Ingredients:

- 1/2 cup raspberries
- 1 banana
- 1 tbsp rolled oats
- 1 scoop whey protein powder, vanilla
- 1 cup water

Preparation:

Prepare all of the ingredients and place them into the Nutribullet. Blend and enjoy.

Roasted Strawberry Protein Smoothie

Ingredients:

- 1 cup fresh strawberries
- 1/2 tbsp raw sugar
- 1/2 cup cottage cheese
- 1/2 cup milk
- 1 tsp chia seeds

Preparation:

Prepare all of the ingredients and place them into the Nutribullet. Blend and enjoy.

Strawberry Banana Quinoa Smoothie

Ingredients:

- 1 banana
- 1 cup vanilla Greek yogurt
- 1/2 cup quinoa
- 2 tbsp honey
- 1 tbsp chia seeds
- 1 tbsp wheat germ
- 2 cups strawberries
- 1 cup vanilla almond milk
- 1 tsp Xantham gum

Preparation:

Prepare all of the ingredients and place them into the Nutribullet. Blend and enjoy.

Super Peach Smoothie

Ingredients:

- 1 cup water
- 1 tbsp flaxseed oil
- 1 peach 6 frozen strawberries
- 1 scoop whey protein

Preparation:

Prepare all of the ingredients and place them into the Nutribullet. Blend and enjoy.

Tropical Pleasure Smoothie

Ingredients:

- 1 cup water
- 1/2 tsp pineapple extract
- 1/2 tsp coconut extract
- 1 tbsp heavy cream
- 1/2 banana
- 1 scoop whey protein
- 4 ice cubes

Preparation:

Prepare all of the ingredients and place them into the Nutribullet. Blend and enjoy.

Vanilla Strawberry Chia Smoothie

Ingredients:

- 1/2 cup strawberries
- 1 scoop protein powder, vanilla
- 1 tsp chia seeds
- 1 cup water

Preparation:

Prepare all of the ingredients and place them into the Nutribullet. Blend and enjoy.

Weight Gain Pro Smoothie

Ingredients:

- 2 scoops whey protein
- 1 cup water (or whole milk)
- 2 bananas
- 1 cup almonds
- 3 tbsp peanut butter

Preparation:

Prepare all of the ingredients and place them into the Nutribullet. Blend and enjoy.

High Protein Ingredients To Add Into Any Shake

- **Avocado**
Protein: 2.3g in 1/2 cup

- **Kale**
Protein: 2.9g in 1 cup

- **Oats**
Protein: 3g in 1/2 cup

- **Walnuts**
Protein: 4.3g in 1 oz

- **Chia Seeds**
Protein: 4.7g in 2 tbsp

- **Pumpkin Seeds**
Protein: 5g in 2 tbsp

- **Cashews**
Protein: 5g in 1 oz

- **Tofu**
Protein: 5g in 6 oz

- **Flax Seeds**
Protein: 5.1g in 1 oz

- **Tahini**
Protein: 5.2g in 2 tbsp

- **Eggs**
Protein: 6g in 1 egg

- **Almonds**
Protein: 6g in 1 oz

- **Almond Butter**
Protein: 7g in 2 tbsp

- **Dairy Milk**
Protein: 8g in 1 cup

- **Peanut Butter**
Protein: 8g in 2 tbsp

- **Quinoa**
Protein: 8g in 1 cup

- **Hemp Seeds**
Protein: 9g in 2 tbsp

- **Greek Yoghurt**
Protein: 10g in 3.5 oz

- **Low-Fat Cottage Cheese**
Protein: 14g in 1/2 cup

- **Hemp Protein Powder**
Protein: 15g in 1 scoop

- **Whey Protein Powder**
Protein: 18gs in 1 scoop

- **Lentils**
Protein: 18gs in 1 cup

- **Soy Protein Powder**
Protein: 22g in 1 scoop

- **Soy Beans**
Protein: 36gs in 3.5 oz

- **Spirulina**
Protein: 58gs in 3.5 oz

CONCLUSION

Making smoothies with a Nutribullet is effective because smoothies are not only delicious but most importantly they are a nutritious snack, not to mention incredibly quick. Imagine being able to customize your protein smoothie shake by selecting the perfect ingredients to make both a healthy and delicious shake. Protein is an essentially building block for muscle and even helps to promote weight loss. Combined with a training regime, one should be able to see great results from drinking the smoothies in Nutribullet Superfood: 40 Protein Packed Power Smoothie Recipes To Help You Lose Weight And Build Lean Muscle.

Thank you again for downloading this book!

I hope this book was able to help you find delicious and nutritious Nutribullet smoothie food recipes.

To hear about Jessica's new books first (and to be notified when there are free promotions), sign up to her New Release Mailing List.

Finally, if you enjoyed this book, please take the time to share your thoughts and post a review on Amazon. It'd be greatly appreciated!

Thank you and good luck!

12765740R00029

Printed in Poland
by Amazon Fulfillment
Poland Sp. z o.o., Wrocław